Beneath the Chaos

Rae Howell

Cover Art by Amanda Evans

For

My children – Thank you for bringing me life and teaching me joy.

"I listened to the old brag of my heart.
                    I am. I am. I am."

-   *Sylvia Plath "The Bell Jar"*
    (Heinemann Publishing, 1963)

Contentment under circumstance.
Accepting life as it is.
Forgetting the dream that pulled you
through each day.

Looking in the mirror and seeing regret in the
face that used to greet you with hope.

What happens when you remember the
dream?
When all you see is failure?
When there is no contentment?

Powerless to change the circumstance.
Desperate to find the girl in the mirror that
had dreams and believed in them.

Perhaps, one day she will come back.
If she can dream it.

The tourniquet is wrapped tight
The vein ready, pulsing
A pinch
A draw
The flood
It flows through
Burning me from the inside
Sweet relief
A deadly poison
I crave it
Desperate for it
You
You brought this upon me
You caused my addiction
One touch and I was taken under

I see her
She's flailing
Desperate for something
I extend my hand
She refuses
She prefers the struggle
Drowning beneath the chaos
The bitterness feeds her soul
A punishment for my sins

The emotions come over me like a wave
Crushing me
Pulling me out to sea
I am helpless to stop it
As the water takes me under,
I hear his voice, telling me to fight
Begging
He is not real
The crushing, pushing, pulling of the angry
sea feels right

I sink into darkness

Finally

Still

It's strange when you notice things have changed

A shift has occurred
You don't feel it or see it until it has already happened

The earth rotates every day, but you do not notice it
Only seeing the effects when day turns into night

I prefer it that way
Oblivious

For some reason I see this shift happening
An outsider watching this life

Powerless to stop it
Not really wanting to stop it

I feel this change
I see it

I should do something about it

I won't

The darkness pulls you in.
You crave a goodbye.
It's the only thing that will save you

What happens when you stay?
You let the darkness overtake you.
It envelops you like a blanket.

Dreams become your alternate reality
The only reality you acknowledge

Two beacons of light pull you through
each day.
They alone bring the light in.
You allow it for fear that without them
you would be lost completely to the dark.

You are far too comfortable in the
darkness.
It feels like home.
A home that welcomes you and is glad to
see you.

The wall that was torn down released me
It put you in bondage
I cannot find it in myself to care

I am free
You are in a personal prison
I laugh at your pain

Jesus forgives
I do not
I find comfort in your discontent

You hid the evil within you
You destroyed innocence

Now I pay the price
Your sins
My blindness

The earthquake hit
The wall crumbled to the ground
I refuse to rebuild it

Too much of life is spent behind a wall
A wall that hides and protects

The earthquake was not caused by me
But, when it hit, it shattered my façade

Terrifying
Exhilarating

When the wall is down and you are
exposed
You can finally see for the first time in
years

You see the misery in the face in the
mirror that was caused by the monster
under the bed

Now, I am free

Even though you push it away
It is still there
Hiding
Waiting
Threatening
It is trying to defeat you
Tear you apart
Better push harder next time

*The poison in her body has permeated and
caused a bitterness that will not be broken*

*Age has caused a filter between the dreams of a
girl and the reality of a woman*

*The wrinkles have no purpose, no happy story
to tell*

*She never wanted to settle,
God had other plans for her*

*Is there a way out?
Can you change the outcome?
Can she get back to the dreams of a girl,
before the doctor tells her it is almost over?*

   No.

I see your face
Eyes closed
Gasping for breath
Your body jerks involuntarily
The pain is consuming you
Taking you under
I can merely watch
Helpless
There is no beauty in this
Ugly
A shallow breath
Your teeth crack
Falling to pieces
I want to end it
End the ugly
I do not remember your beauty
The soft lines of your face
The tenderness of your smile
All I see is ugly

I see my reflection
I see you
I am terrified

  Where I used to see beauty
  I now see deterioration
  I am morphing into you

The skin peeling away into grey
Your light does not shine through me
My darkness has overtaken your beauty
Fading away into the black heart I possess

    Where did you go?
    I fear I will never find you again
    Would you even know me now?
    Would you want to?

Every day, more and more of you disappears from my mind.

The process of eliminating you is torturous.

I cannot survive while you still live within me.

The pain is unbearable.

I methodically takes parts of you and crush them.

Your smile.

Your laugh.

Your hands.

Your eyes.

Gone.

But, I cannot demolish your words.

They are slowly killing me

They will not leave me be.

Once so beautiful and inspiring, they are now a toxin.

A toxin I cannot rid myself of.

You left your words in my heart, pumping the blood through my veins.

You left them on my body, sweetly burning my flesh.

Then you vanished, leaving me to pick up the pieces.

You are gone.

Your words stay.

The blood does not flow anymore.

The flesh rots. The words stay.

It is quite possible that at the beginning of autumn I am at my lowest.

The changing leaves,
*   the cooler weather,*
*   the crisp air.*

Another year has passed,
*   seasons have changed,*
*   and yet I am still in the same place.*

*   Alone.*

Once so full of beauty and promise.
Abandoned and left to rot.

Reconstruction takes time.
Effort.

The beauty is still there.
You must work harder to find it this time.

In the quiet hours of the night my mind is the loudest.

Constantly screaming out the insecurities the day tries to hide.

The words pour out of my soul during the night.
      Nobody can hear my honesty.

As I take my last breath
My eyes focus on you
Your eyes go from rage to horror

As I take my last breath
My body no longer feels pain
Your body is rigid, covered in blood

As I take my last breath
I hear nothing, silence is peace
You are screaming

As I take my last breath
Lavender fills my senses
You smell the burning flesh

As I take my last breath
My memories are filled with love
You only feel hate

As I take my last breath
I love you
You only love yourself

As I take my last breath
I forgive you
You will never forgive yourself

As I take my last breath
I am, at last, alive
You are dead

Restless? ~~always~~

Broken? ~~a little~~

Hopeful? ~~never~~

Today I begin
A new passion creeping in
Today I will find a place where fear and
lies melt away
I am determined
I am broken pieces of who I want to be
I will
I want
I am

The night is when I feel it the most
Failures creep in
The wasted dreams
The solitude

I revel in these feelings
It is my paradise
It is the only way I know I'm alive
I welcome the night

In the dark, I find my inspiration
The fear of rejection engages my senses
The act of rejection makes the ink flow on to
paper

Tonight, I write

Insecurity
Sorrow
Heartbreak
Fear

Sometimes, it takes just one person to help you overcome
Sometimes, you have to give yourself over to faith
Sometimes, you have to face the ugly that you have made up inside your own mind

You don't have to be insecure
You are worthy
You don't have to hold on to the sorrow
Your heart is strong
Open it
You don't have to be afraid
Face the monster you created

Sometimes, you write to convince yourself
Sometimes, you actually believe it

The Book is open.
She knows every word.
The rules of life.
She abides, studies, believes.

A life taken in agony.
Where are You?

The knife digs in deeper.
Where are You?

Your faithful servant dies in flames.
Where are You?

A violent touch steals innocence.
Where are You?

Shadows in the dark.
Where are You?

The Book is closed.
She knows every word.
The rules of life.
She abides, questions, believes.

A dark stare
A love lost
A hope dies
A touch is all it would take
A fire within coming alive
A forgotten emotion
Do you feel it?
Do you remember?

His body is a temple
I stand at the alter
Desperate for a touch
Mesmerized by the soul behind the eyes
Desperate to climb inside
Begging him to let me in
Shattered pieces of a man envelop my being
I embrace it
Clinging to the shards
They pierce my skin
Blood flowing out of my body on to his
I give myself completely
A moth to a flame
Burning, screaming
My body aches for a touch
A touch that will end me
I welcome it
His body is a temple
I fall at his feet
Take me
Break me

You have the power to crush me
You never asked for it
My desire for you is incomparable to any other
Beyond the physical
A terrifying connection
Liberating
My fantasy brought into my reality

Tread lightly

I miss you
I want to kiss you
I want your hands in my hair
I want my hands on your body
I want to see your face
I want your voice in my ears
I want you

Today, I want to feel optimism
      Despite the darkness that swarms
      in my head

I want
I want

Today, I crave beauty and light
      Despite the ugly I see in the mirror

I crave
I crave

Today, I am desolate

The dead inside had come alive
The sound of your voice sparked life
Your touch on my body awakened
something wild inside
Your mouth was the escape I always
needed, craved

You took it all away

I want to know what you taste like now
I want to know how your body feels
above me
I still crave your touch
You are right in front of me, you deny me

I wait

The dawn was coming
I could see you on the horizon

A new day
Awakened

The freshness of the air hit me
Hope welled up inside

I saw you in the distance
I've waited for this moment

You are the dawn
You are the light

As you feel the world start to tremble

I will hold you steady

Your eyes never quite see me
Your hands do not touch me
Your mouth speaks half truths

My eyes see what you try to hide
My hands melt away on your skin
My mouth tells you all of my truths

I lay myself out before you
You do not accept me

Can we fall away from this world
Fall to a place of you and I

My heart never ached, before you
The moment you kiss me goodbye
I am lost
A part of me goes with you
I do not feel alive unless your touch is
imminent
You have taken your very being and
entwined it with mine
I will not survive should you pull away

Do not mock the exposed heart

It deteriorates quickly without you

The dagger pierces the flesh.
The blood flows.
The heart is open.
Can you feel it?
Do you see me pouring out?
Is it enough?
My heart laid out before you.
A slow death.
Pain infiltrates everywhere.
I don't mind.
It means you are real.
I allowed you in.
I allowed you to tear me apart.
You hold the power.
You always have.
I cannot remain strong while you hold
my beating heart.
Your hand starts to flex.
Tighter.
Tighter.
Your eyes are not focused on me anymore.
You stare at my flesh in your hands.
"I don't want this anymore." are the last
words I hear.
You crush me.
I welcome it.
Goodbye, my love.

The destruction is imminent

The aftermath unknown

He invades my dreams
My every thought
I am haunted by his voice
I feel his touch in the night
His hands burning on my skin
His words in my ears
Every night I am tortured
Every morning I wake with a memory

I am opened
I show you the depths of myself
You demand it
You show me nothing of yourself
I beg you to let me in
I am discarded
You demand it

Your hands, once like fire on my body, have gone cold

You took away the blood that flows through me

I beg for a touch

I fall to my knees

Please

I want your body to burn with mine

I want to be consumed by your touch

You reject

You run

I am vile in your eyes

My body turning grey without your touch

I am not what you desire

Your body does not tremble for my touch

I do not bring you to the brink of insanity

To me, you are everything

To you, I am nothing

Absence doesn't make the heart grow fonder.

It makes it easier to forget.

Did you forget?

I am still here.

Drowning.

What is this thing that sleeps inside of me?
It rips at my soul
Tears down my mind
I want you to rescue me
Save me from myself
I want you to pull me out of my torturous mind
But, my smile
My laugh
My eyes
They will never allow you to know that I need
saving
And you do not look beyond the surface

A one sided emotion
I do not fit into your world
What am I to you?
A burden?
A lost desire?
A new beginning?
A distraction?
Nothing.

Tell me you ache for me as I do for you.

Tell me that a part of you feels empty without my presence.

Tell me that I am not alone.

Tell me that your mouth is not full of lies.

Tell me that I am enough.

Tell me all of these things before you tear me to pieces.

The ache is slow.

It builds from deep within.

Is it visible from the outside?

Do I hide it?

A world without you is coming for me.

I cannot bear the thought of my soul without you.

You brought me in, introduced me to the light.

Now, I am cast back into the darkness.

"I love you" falls off your tongue with ease.

Without reason, I believe your words.

My desperation for you blinds me on the outside.

Deep within I know the truth.

"I love you" falls my tongue with ease.

It is the most truth I have ever spoken.

I used to dream to escape reality
Now reality has chased away my dreams
If you run, I will let you

Suffocating under the heaviness of words left unsaid.

My darkness hides behind the wall I am reconstructing.

The door closes a little more every day

Once, I believed you could bring the light,

Now, I fear, it will be too much for you to bear.

Stay is all I can ask of you

Show me you mean what you say.

Show me that you desire to crawl inside

Show me that you are worthy of this darkness

My wall is visible

Yours is hidden

I open the door

You stay behind the glass

Fleeting moments of self-assurance.
I am too much on the other side.
I want you to burn for me as I do you.
A futile dream.

How long until you end my suffering?
I see your eyes full of rage.
I hear your voice dripping with spite.
You taunt me.
Circling me like prey.
One sudden move and you will do me in.
I am forever in fear.
Do it.
Do not give kindness and then take it away.
Do not make me hope.
Do not promise an unavailable heart.
One.
Two.
Three.
I make my move.

I write to find myself.
I write to lose myself.
I write to keep myself sane.
I write to keep you alive.
I write to keep you away.
I write to keep you close.
I write because of you.
I write for you.

226
307
419

Forever Altered

I write letters that come from within, telling you the secrets of my heart.

Can you feel my heart beating with the words I cannot speak?

My heart belongs to none but you.

You will find it
That ugly part of me
The part that makes everyone leave
I don't even know what it is
It scares me
I had built such a wall around myself
Protection
You showed up, out of nowhere
Made a door and walked in
I have opened my battered heart
I let you in
Please be real
Please give me the chance to show I'm worthy
I'm good
Please don't run
There is beauty in this ugly
Please stay and find it
Beneath the rubble of the past that I crawled
out of, I found you

Faith in yourself.

Faith in him.

Faith in love.

The door was opened

Unwillingly

Trust was given

Unwillingly

A heart exposed

Unwillingly

I love you

Willingly